DIY Cannabis Extracts

*Cannabis Preparation Made Simple.
The Essential Guide to Making Medical
Marijuana Extracts At Home
(2022 Guide for All)*

Ryan Griffith

Content list

Chapter 9

How to make Edibles,

Part II:

Further Exploration

Chapter 10

How to Make Hash

Chapter 11

How to Make Bubble Hash

Chapter 12

How to Make Kief

Chapter 13

How to Make Rosin & "Do a Dab"

Chapter 14

Looking Forward to the Future

INTRODUCTION

Cannabis has recently gained popularity as a treatment for various ailments and illnesses. The once-shady perception of this healing herb has shifted from "dangerous drug" to "effective." It is a medicinal plant that has been used to treat minor ailments as from minor ailments like arthritis and sore muscles to major ones like glaucoma and diabetes. CBD, the cannabis miracle compound, can help with insomnia (Cannabidiol), has helped a number of cancer patients by providing an all-natural method of stopping this global killer. The sweet, aromatic herb can be consumed in a variety of ways. Cannabis-based new technology can take the form of a pill, a liquid, or a spray. Vape pens, tinctures, and a variety of other forms are available. Extracts are an excellent choice how to make use of this miracle plant Cannabis extracts include oils and other products.

Products that have been reduced in size make them smokeless but still medicine that works. One dose can be as little as a drop, which can be concealed in any beverage or favorite dish. Cannabis extracts are still available. Be smoked for those who prefer it (the dab is a popular method). An example of one of these extracts can be found here;

Cannabis extracts will have the same properties when made professionally. They have the same characteristics as the buds from which they were created, giving any use of the authentic experience of each person's uniqueness. However, these products are not inexpensive and making them can be hazardous if you don't know what you're doing. Cannabis is a huge market these days, and the new extraction methods are helping to expand it. Methods have grown in popularity among a large number of users. This as demand for extracts has increased; prices have risen predictably skyrocketed. You should be able to do so if you use this book as a resource. This cost, as well as the safety risks associated with cannabis extracts, can be significantly reduced. You will be able to do so by the end of this book. You could potentially become a manufacturer yourself!

In this book, we begin each chapter with a brief discussion of the extract, the supplies required, and the recommended safety precautions. Then we add diligent and systematic instructions to ensure success. In no time, you'll be producing your cannabis extracts!

The first chapter will go over the health benefits of using cannabis extracts and posing potential health risks in relation to the plant. The second chapter focuses on acquiring plant material from others, which is a critical step in producing cannabis extracts. The third chapter will go over how to grow cannabis briefly yourself after you are aware of the many potential health risks, cannabis's health benefits, as well as what you'll need to. Once you begin, you will be sent on a wonderful journey of discovery knowledge! You will have learned how to make butane after reading this book. Rick Simpson oil, hash oil, tinctures, cannabutter, edibles such as brownies and cookies (there are two chapters dedicated to this art), Hash, bubble hash, rosin (or dabs), and kief are all examples of cannabis products. Each chapter describes what each extract is and how to use it. How to use it, and most importantly, how to make it. Are you prepared to save colossal sums of money and become a herb craftsman in the department of extraction? So, let's get this party started!

Chapter 1

Potential Health Benefits.

What Makes Cannabis Tick?

The impending introduction of cannabis into the medical world has many drug manufacturers trembling. Compared to other, more conventional drugs, this all-natural remedy has fewer symptoms and side effects and is simple to make at home. All you require are resources in the form of knowledge and small gardens.

One such obvious comparison is the comparison of formal pain relievers to cannabis. Many opium-based drugs used to treat pain cause withdrawal symptoms when the drug is no longer required. This will never happen with cannabis because it does not cause physical dependence in people (though a slight mental dependency has been reported, depending on the user).

If a person takes too many pain relievers, they will most likely overdose, necessitating a trip to the hospital and possibly death. However, if one consumes too much cannabis, they may simply experience an empty refrigerator or an unplanned nap or two.

Nonetheless, there are some unpleasant side effects and some health risks associated with cannabis use. However, the benefits of using cannabis, particularly extracts, far outweigh the risks. First, let us investigate this enchanted plant and briefly discuss what makes it a remedy.

Without delving into complicated chemistry, we will explain what cannabis is and what gives the plant its medicinal properties in a simple, easy-to-understand format. Are you prepared?

THC (Tetrahydrocannabinol) and CBD are the two main chemical compounds that make cannabis a healing plant (Cannabidiol). Cannabis, when combined with both chemical compounds, has proven to be a powerful healer for many people!

THC: Ease Chronic Pain with a Helpful Strain

THC is unquestionably the most well-known compound in cannabis. THC is the substance that causes you to "feel good." THC has been tested for pain-relieving effects by researchers, and the results have shown that it is extremely capable of relieving chronic pain in each test. Researchers Igor Grant, J. Hampton Atkinson, Ben Gouaux, and Barth Wilsey tested the use of THC against placebos and codeine (an opiate) in the article Medical Marijuana: Clearing the Smoke (2012).

THC was found to be effective in reducing chronic pain in their study. It worked just as well as codeine but without the adverse side effects, such as body-bending withdrawals.

THC did, however, have some psychoactive effects, but they were usually minor and never long-lasting. Dry mouth, fatigue, muscle weakness, light-headedness, and slight palpitations were among the other side effects. These effects were largely insignificant, occurring in fewer cases of newer users. At the end of the day, THC is an excellent option for relieving chronic pain in general. THC can also be used to treat a variety of other ailments.

It has helped people suffering from depression, insomnia, eating disorders, and anxiety.

CBD: Cancer Be Dead!

CBD is a more recent discovery, and its ability to produce miracles in cancer cases has been discovered.

CBD, unlike THC, has no psychoactive effects. You will not experience the same euphoric high that THC does if you take CBD. On the other hand, this chemical compound has become well-known for its ability to destroy malignant, cancerous cells.

CBD introduces oxygen into cancer cells, causing calcium to accumulate and stifle cancer cell growth. Cancer develops in stages, and as it grows older, it requires more nutrients to survive. If the cancer is unable to obtain the required nutrients as it grows, it will eventually die and become a non-malignant tumor.

THC & CBD: What A Team!

Because cannabis contains both THC and CBD, it has become a powerful weapon in the fight against cancer, as these two miraculous compounds attack only the cancerous cells. It is debatable whether or not this incredible team will completely cure cancer. Nonetheless, it is widely acknowledged that, at the very least, it can play a role in the battle.

Dennis Hill, a biochemist who claims to have beaten stage four cancer with cannabis oil, explains how the two work together in his article "How Cannabinoids Kill Cancer." THC deprives the cancer cell of energy by disrupting its mitochondria. CBD then enters the picture and floods the cell with calcium. THC also interferes with calcium metabolism in cancer cells.

As a result, as CBD floods the cell with calcium, the cell cannot expel the calcium due to THC. As a result, the cell dies or becomes stagnant. To put it another way, imagine the THC encasing the cancer cell in a bubble and then the CBD attacking it. With the news that this combination effectively combats cancerous cells, an increasing number of people are turning to various sources of cannabis to treat their cancer.

Sativa (THC) & India (CBD)

Of course, cannabis is also used recreationally to relax and relieve stress. It can also be used to relieve arthritis pain or to help you fall asleep if you have trouble sleeping. And if you're suffering from a lack of appetite, cannabis will have you eating in no time!

Sativa has a higher THC content, giving the user a stimulated, heavy feeling — ideal for sleeping and eating disorders. Sativa is also used to treat chronic pain, such as severe back injuries and broken bones.

Indica is much higher in CBD content, providing a lighter mental euphoria and aiding in the treatment of anxiety and internal inflammatory issues. Indica can be used in the opposite way for eating because it is known to suppress appetite. As a result, it is also recommended for the treatment of obesity.

Remember this when using these strains for recreational purposes: Sativa produces a physical high, whereas Indica produces a mental high. It's easy to distinguish between the two by remembering Sativa as "sleepy-time cannabis" and Indica as "day-time cannabis."

Why Cannabis Extracts?

Cannabis extracts are generally a healthier way to consume cannabis. Smoking is bad for you in the long run because it promotes unhealthy blood flow and breathing problems. However, by experimenting with various extraction methods, one can achieve the desired cannabis effect in a variety of ways.

Vapors emit no fumes and are thus gentle on the lungs, as well as enjoyable and highly effective. Oils and tinctures can be applied to almost anything, and they completely eliminate the presence of smoke. Other extracts, such as cannabutter, can be spread on toast or mixed into a cake recipe.

Some extracts do contain smoke, but because they are reductions of the cannabis plant, they produce a small amount of smoke because no burning vegetation is involved.

These extracts include hash, kief, and the very popular rosin. Although these extracts are typically smoked, they emit significantly fewer fumes, resulting in a healthier cannabis experience.

It is strongly advised that if you are using cannabis to treat breathing-related ailments, such as COPD (Chronic obstructive pulmonary disease), where cannabis acts as an anti-inflammatory, that you do not smoke it, even in vapor form. The same is true if you are treating lung cancer. This is where extracts like oils, butters, and tinctures come into play. However, before you can begin making these wonderful products, you must first acquire the necessary materials. The first and most important component is the plant material.

Chapter 2

Acquiring Plant Material. Part I:

Outside Sources

We've established what cannabis extracts are and how they can benefit users so far. Now, we'll go over one of the most critical aspects of producing cannabis extracts: obtaining plant material. There are two approaches to this, so we will divide this aspect of cannabis extract production into two chapters. This first chapter will go over cannabis laws and how to get plant material from three different outside sources. Medical dispensaries, retailers, and cannabis farmers are the three sources.

I know you want to get started on your cannabis extracts as soon as possible. However, it is critical that you are aware of cannabis laws. These will be determined by the state or country in which you reside.

Furthermore, if your state does not support the use of cannabis, either medicinally or recreationally, you should not attempt to make any of these cannabis extracts at this time. The last thing we want is for you to get into legal trouble!

The following is a quick rundown of cannabis laws in the United States. If you are visiting from another country, please familiarize yourself with your home country's laws and regulations.

Laws: Medical Cannabis

Cannabis has many healing properties for those who prefer it to other forms of treatment for illnesses and ailments.

However, if you intend to use medical cannabis, you should be aware of some guidelines and rules.

If you travel to different states, the medical marijuana laws may differ, but the basic rules remain the same:

If a physician has given you permission to use medical marijuana, you can do so in the privacy of your own home.

Using cannabis legally is analogous to using any prescription drug; you cannot drive while using cannabis, and you are not permitted to use cannabis in public.

As a medicinal cannabis user, you have access to a number of dispensaries, also known as "Cannabis Clubs" by many. If you are a caregiver for someone who uses medical cannabis, you are legally permitted to handle the plant. However, you are not permitted to use it. You can grow cannabis as a medical cannabis patient, and you can do so collectively. Growing cannabis is usually permitted between 4 and 12 plants, depending on the state's regulations. Buds can typically be consumed in quantities ranging from 1 to 8 ounces.

Even if cannabis is legal in your state for medical purposes, your state's medical cannabis laws are still flawed.

Cannabis is not legal in the United States, so the federal government can still prosecute you if you grow it.

However, there is an unwritten rule with the federal government that if you do not pose a threat to society (for example, growing massive amounts of cannabis with the intent to sell), the federal government will most likely not bother you. As a result, it is recommended in medical states to grow no more than 8-12 plants per person in order to avoid legal issues. In states where medical cannabis has been legalized, people have been granted the right to grow collectively. This means that if you and a friend both have legal documents, you can grow medical cannabis together, effectively doubling the number of plants. Again, this can be a risky business, and one should proceed with caution when growing large amounts of cannabis, as the federal government has a penchant for busting large crop owners — even if their intent is solely for personal use. When growing in collective groups, it is recommended that no more than 100 plants be grown.

As of this writing, the following states and territories permit the legal use of medical cannabis: Alaska, Arizona, Arkansas, California, Colorado, Connecticut, Delaware, Florida, Hawaii, Illinois, Main, Maryland, Massachusetts, Michigan, Montana, Nevada, New Hampshire, New Jersey, New York, North Dakota, Ohio, Oregon, Pennsylvania, Rhode Island, Vermont, Washington and Washington, D.C.

If you live in one of these states, you have access to medical cannabis; however, you must be diligent and cautious, as federal regulations still strongly support zero-tolerance.

Laws: Recreational Purposes

As the benefits of cannabis become more widely recognized and accepted in society, many states have begun to legalize its use for recreational purposes as well.

The simplest way to comprehend these laws is to contrast them with existing alcohol laws.

Cannabis products, like alcohol, are sold in local stores in states where cannabis is legal for recreational use. Cannabis, like alcohol, cannot be consumed in public and cannot be driven while under the influence. Like alcohol, one can make their own and sell it to other users whenever they want. Cannabis, like alcohol, requires a legal drinking age of 21. Almost every aspect of recreational cannabis laws is similar to alcohol laws. Nonetheless, in states that have only recently legalized the recreational use of cannabis, there are still some issues and loose ends to be resolved.

Despite the fact that cannabis has recently been legalized in California, cannabis enthusiasts are still unable to purchase the herb unless they purchase it from a grower or the buds are bestowed upon them by someone who has a medical card. So far, the most unresolved issue is how law enforcement will measure and determine cannabis consumption in relation to operating a vehicle. Most states that have already legalized cannabis for recreational purposes have zero tolerance for cannabis use while driving.

The following states have legalized cannabis for recreational use: Washington (state), Oregon, State of California, Nevada, Colorado, Massachusetts and Maine.

As this list clearly shows, legalizing medical cannabis for recreational purposes is still a long way from becoming widely accepted on a national scale.

Obtaining Plant Material

As previously stated, cannabis can be obtained from medical dispensaries, stores (only in cases where recreational use has been legalized and implemented for an extended period of time), or cannabis farmers. In the following section, we will go over some pointers and suggestions for obtaining plant material from each of these sources.

Medical Dispensaries and Retailers

Making extracts from flowers can be very expensive depending on what you require in your extract if you plan to obtain plant material from a medical dispensary or a retailer. However, trimmings, a mixture of leaves and flowers left over from a harvest, are reasonably priced at medical dispensaries and convenience stores. This is also a good ingredient for extracts because it produces good results at a reasonable price.

Purchasing the actual flowers and producing your extracts can be costly, but the end result will be worth it. If you want to make a more potent cannabis extract with a strong presence of the strain's character, you're better off buying the extract from a medical dispensary or retailer; it's more cost-effective.

Farmers

Your best bet for obtaining plant material from an outside source is to have a farmer friend or a friend of a farmer friend. When farmers harvest, they usually have a lot of trimmings or small flowers known as "budlets." Another reason to seek out a farmer is that they typically sell their cannabis at a much lower price than clubs and retailers. By locating a farmer, you can bypass the middleman and begin producing cannabis extracts in no time!

Although the three methods discussed here are quick and easy ways to obtain plant material for cannabis extracts, they are a little more expensive — especially if you want to make higher-grade products. There is a way to avoid this, but it takes time and effort. However, with hard work and dedication, you will have more than enough plant material to work with.

Growing your own cannabis plants is by far the most efficient way to obtain raw material if you want to produce large amounts of flowers for a specialized extract or if you want to produce large amounts of mid-grade extracts.

Chapter 3

Obtaining Plant Material Part II: Growing Cannabis

We discussed how to obtain plant material from outside sources in the previous chapter. Although you can obtain flowers and leaves from outside sources, it can be prohibitively expensive. Yes, obtaining plant material from a third party is much faster and more convenient, but the quality of your extracts will be far from optimal when compared to growing your own plant material. It takes time, a lot of work, and dedication, but the end result is well worth it.

In the previous chapter, we also learned that growing cannabis is legal in certain states and territories.

Some require medical use and others completely legalize the herb for recreational purposes.

Let us remember that growing cannabis outside of these designated states and territories is illegal and can result in disaster.

Now that we've established that, let's go over the fundamentals of growing the most delectable cannabis.

Where Does One Obtain Seeds, or Clones?

Seeds and clones are not challenging to come by. Seeds can be purchased from a medical dispensary, a store that specializes in seed production, or a farmer. You may also find some seeds in your buds. However, not all seeds are usable because when growing cannabis buds, you want a female plant. With seeds, it can take weeks to determine whether the plant is male or female.

Male plants, which have small seed pods around stem junctions, produce hemp with no THC and significantly lower levels of CBD than female plants. Female plants with tiny hairs around stem junctions are the ones you want because they produce a lot of buds. Seeds are inexpensive, but they can be risky.

The use of clones is a safer bet. If you buy or make your

own clone, it will undoubtedly be a female. Clones can be purchased from the same establishments and outlets mentioned previously, but they are more expensive depending on the age of the plant. In addition, if you already have a female plant, you can easily clone it. This is accomplished simply by clipping a branch from your plant and placing it in soil, where it will grow its own roots. When doing this, always use sterilized sharp pruners or scissors, and cut the branch at a 45-degree angle right below new growth that has grown 5-8 inches. Let's grow some cannabis now that we have our plants!

Outdoor Cannabis

This is the most basic method of growing cannabis, and it is highly recommended that you try it before venturing into indoor grow operations. Indoor grow operations should only be undertaken by experienced growers due to the increased number of variables and difficulties. There are numerous methods for growing cannabis outside, but since this is not the focus of this book, we will only cover the fundamentals here.

To begin, you must be familiar with your surroundings. Cannabis grows best in temperatures ranging from 55 to 86 degrees Fahrenheit (12 to 30 degrees Celsius). Furthermore, cannabis prefers a temperate climate, as storms and strong winds can harm her majesty. Nonetheless, cannabis has been dubbed "weed" for a reason: it can grow almost anywhere and will produce buds if the following seasonal guidelines are followed: Begin at the end of spring and finish at the beginning of fall. This is determined by how you begin, as seeds require more time than clones.

Second, finding the right location to grow your cannabis is difficult. Again, this will be determined by where you live, as a healthy plant requires 5-6 hours of direct sunlight per day. If the weather is warm, grow your cannabis in an area that receives early morning light to avoid burning it. In colder climates, provide your cannabis with light that comes later in the day for a warmer and happier plant. Also, keep security in mind, as sticky fingers and rolling eyes are known to find their way into cannabis gardens sooner or later. Maintain the safety of your plants!

Third, you should concentrate on the soil. There are many different soil cocktails that are effective for cannabis growth, but silty soil is the most basic and easiest to use. It allows for good aeration and effectively retains heat for the roots. This soil is rich in nutrients and can be found at the bottom of lakebeds and old rivers.

Cannabis fertilizers are specialized fertilizers made

specifically for cannabis cultivation. It is recommended to use super soil (organic pre-fertilized soil) if you do not want to worry about soil repair. This is a more expensive option, but it works wonders in the garden.

Water is the fifth element. Water your plant as needed; as an adult, flowering female can require up to ten gallons of water per day! Also, ensure that the water is clean and free of chemicals like chlorine; tap water should always be tested beforehand. Keep her hydrated, and she'll produce the best crop for your cannabis-extract requirements.

Finally, keep bugs away from your plants. Again, there are numerous methods for protecting your plants from pesky insects, but the most natural method is to fight fire with fire! Purchase a box of ladybugs or praying mantises from your local gardening store. These helpful soldiers will not eat your cannabis; instead, they will eat the other tiny bugs that will eat up your precious plants.

Pay close attention to the little white hairs on your buds when harvesting. When about half of them turn an orange-brown color, it's time to harvest.

Indoor Cannabis

Indoor cannabis cultivation is a more complicated science, with methods ranging from simple procedures to eloquent displays of art. This science's development has resulted in pages and pages of techniques, formulas, and equipment.

It is advised that you locate a reliable source that specializes in this field. However, we will quickly go over the fundamental knowledge you will need to grow cannabis in your home to see if it is a viable option for you successfully.

Supplies Needed

A high-pressure sodium (HPS) light, a fan, a growing tent (or you may create your own confinement), agricultural fertilizer (the same as in outdoor operations will suffice), and a stopwatch (this will prove extremely handy).

You can begin after you have set up your indoor grow room. Begin by germinating your seeds. They only need soil and water to do this.

When they appear, you should begin feeding them light.

This is where the timer comes in. Connect your HPS light to your timer and set it to turn on for 18 hours and turn off for 6 hours. As the vegetation stage begins, your cannabis will require this light cycle for up to 4 weeks. Remember that cannabis is a thirsty plant, so make sure to provide your plant with plenty of clean water.

She will enter the flower stage once she has finished vegging. When this occurs, set your timer for 12 hours on and 12 hours off. This will result in a thicket of luscious, pungent cannabis flowers.

Spider mites are another thing to keep in mind when growing indoors. By wrapping their silky webs around your plant's leaves, they will suffocate it. The use of neem oil is a sure way to get rid of these little pests naturally. If you notice spider mites on your plant, act quickly because they are notorious for destroying entire crops! Now that we've looked at both outdoor and indoor methods, you're ready to pick your favorite. Growing cannabis is a lot of work and takes time, but once you get into a routine and can easily produce gardens, the benefits will last a lifetime. Once you've mastered the art of cannabis cultivation, you'll never run out of material for your extracts again!

Chapter 4

How to Make Butane Hash Oil (BHO)

Honey Oil

BHO (Butane Hash Oil), also known as "honey oil" by many, is one of the oldest cannabis extracts available. This potent oil contains some CBD, but it is also extremely high in THC, so use with caution. THC and CBD chemicals are extracted from the plant, leaving all vegetation behind and settling in pure, aromatic oil. BHO can be smoked in a variety of ways. The most traditional method, however, is to apply it directly to a lush, green bowl of cannabis.

If smoking BHO is your preferred method of use, it is recommended that you do so for recreational purposes only, as smoking can exacerbate certain health problems in the long run. However, if you want to use BHO to treat medical issues, you can buy vaporizers that convert the oil into vapor, which is easier on the lungs.

In short, the process of producing BHO is straightforward: butane separates the cannabinoids from the plant matter and passes it through a strainer. The end result is a mixture of butane and cannabis goodness. Butane will evaporate on its own over time, but there are some methods we can use to speed up the process. It appears simple enough, but there are some supplies you'll need and some safety precautions to keep in mind.

Safety and Such

There aren't many safety precautions to be aware of when making BHO on a smaller scale. Make certain that the materials are of high quality so that they do not malfunction and that you are in an area with adequate airflow (so butane does not build up). It is also advised to wear a mask to avoid inhaling harmful fumes. You should also wear safety glasses just in case; it's better to be safe than sorry.

Now that we've covered the safety precautions, let's get started on making our own honey oil!

Supplies Needed

Cannabis: The higher the quality of your cannabis flowers, the higher the quality of your BHO. However, you can make this extract from leaves and clippings, which is a method that people have been using for years to turn trash into gold.

Butane: As you might expect from the product's name (Butane Hash Oil), butane is an important component in this equation. It is suggested that a 10 oz. can be used for every ounce of plant material.

Glass Extraction Tube: A glass extraction tube is required for this process. These range in price from $40 to $100, depending on size and manufacturer. To avoid cracking glass, it is strongly advised to purchase a long-lasting extraction tube.

Pyrex Dishes: One medium and one large Pyrex dish are required. This heat-resistant glassware will be useful, and you can find it almost anywhere.

Razor Blade Scraper: This item is simple to obtain and can be purchased at any hardware store such as Ace or Home Depot.

Concentrate Container: These small containers will save you from wasting your valuable cannabis oil and will keep it fresh and potent. They are made of a nonstick material and can be purchased at a smoke shop for about ten to fifteen dollars.

(Option 1) Electric Heating Pad: This common household item is available at any drug store. If you select this option, you will not require the following item.

(Option 2) Vacuum Purging System: This is the more expensive option. Nonetheless, it improves the efficiency of the manufacturing process. If you use a vacuum purge, you will not require a heating pad. Now that we've covered all of the materials you'll need, let's get started on making some butane hash oil!

The Process

The first step will be to fill your extraction tube with cannabis plant material. The plant material you use must be completely dry and densely packed to prevent air bubbles from forming. If your extractor tube did not come with a filter screen, you could replace it with a mesh coffee filter at the larger end of the tube. When your cannabis is tightly packed, and your screen is securely fastened to the bottom, you are ready to begin.

Step 2: Cannabinoids Extraction

Take your medium Pyrex dish and set it on a sturdy surface.

Place the extraction tube on top of the dish, with the screen side down. Insert the butane nozzle into the smaller hole on top of the extractor and fill the tube with butane. The gold liquid will start dripping through the screen and onto the medium Pyrex dish. Continue this process until the liquid no longer resembles gold. This means that all of the cannabinoids in the flowers or leaves have been depleted.

Step 3 Evaporation .

You should now have golden oil and butane in a medium Pyrex dish. The next step is to separate the dangerous butane from the newer method. The former is less expensive than the latter, but the process is more time-consuming. To avoid harmful fumes, you should make sure the area you are in is well ventilated and wear any type of air filtering mask.

You must begin the same way, regardless of whether you use an old-fashioned or modern method. Fill the large Pyrex dish halfway with hot water and set the medium dish inside. The evaporation process will begin with the heating of molecules, and butane will begin to flee from the oil.

The traditional method: If you're using a heating pad, place it under the large Pyrex dish and set it to high to keep the water hot all the time. The evaporation process should only take 60-90 minutes.

The modern approach: The process will be much faster if you use a vacuum purge. Simply place the vacuum purge over the two dishes and allow it to do its work! Between 10 and 20 minutes, you'll have butane-free, delicious honey oil!

When the oil no longer has a murky appearance, evaporation has occurred. To be sure, carefully light a flame next to fresh hash oil. If it ignites, you should keep the evaporation process going.

Step 4: Keep It and Enjoy It

Using your razor blade scraper, scrape away any remaining oil in the dish. Transfer it immediately to a concentrate container to keep your honey oil fresh, tasty, and potent for a long time. Finally, it's time to have fun!

Chapter 5

How to Make Rick Simpson Oil (RSO)

Story of a Healer

Rick Simpson has spent the last ten years advocating for and disseminating information about the use of medical cannabis to treat ailments ranging from minor to severe. Simpson began self-medicating with cannabis in 1997 to treat a head injury he had sustained. Rick Simpson's personal outcomes from treating his head injury changed his life, and as time passed, he began to share his story of recovery, changing the lives of many along the way.

Rick Simpson successfully treated skin cancer with his cannabinoid oil recipe in 2003. With his homemade miracle oil, this visionary began assisting people suffering from ailments ranging from cancer to HIV

. Aside from the recipe, what distinguished Rick Simpson's magical cannabis oil from others was the method of application.

Traditionally, most people would smoke cannabis oils. However, Rick Simpson argued that this was ineffective for treating serious medical issues. Simpson instead advised people to apply the oil directly to their skin or ingest it with food or beverages. It wasn't long before RSO (Rick Simpson Oil) was widely accepted by Canadians, as near-miraculous stories of healing began to emerge across the country.

Unfortunately, because cannabis was illegal in Canada, Rick Simpson's practice was eventually terminated by authorities. To the dismay of many, he was charged with a variety of marijuana trafficking counts, and many of the people who relied on his magical oil were denied treatment. Nonetheless, Rick Simpson remained steadfast in his belief and continued to spread the word.

There was a new healer in the medical world, but many people were disappointed to learn that it was cannabis.

Since then, the world has changed dramatically, thanks in large part to the internet's informational nature. Cannabis is no longer simply described as a "dangerous drug," as younger generations have brought with them open minds.

Rick Simpson is one of the primary reasons why so many people have come to view cannabis in a new light.

His magical oil, which is made up of cannabinoids extracted solely through the use of solvents (alcohol being the most common), has played an important role in shaping the enlightenment surrounding this beneficial compound.

RSO marches forward, stronger than ever, into the new era, as this medical asset continues to produce miracles all over the world. Are you interested in learning how to make your own healing oil?

Safety and Such

Before we begin, we want to emphasize that this method of producing cannabis extracts should be approached with caution because it is extremely flammable. Wear protective eyewear as well as long sleeves and an air filtering mask.

Make sure the area where you build has good airflow and a nearby fan to help with ventilation. DO NOT SMOKE IN THE AREA OF PRODUCTION, AND STAY AWAY FROM ANY TYPE OF STOVETOP OR OTHER HEAT SOURCE THAT MAY SPARK A FLAME. Again, this is a highly flammable process. First and foremost, safety!

Now that you've considered all of the necessary safety precautions, let's make a list of what you'll need to get started.

Supplies Needed

- **Cannabis**

Make an effort to consume at least one ounce of cannabis. Using more than one pound of plant material is not recommended when making RSO at home. Also, please make certain that it is completely dry!

- **Plastic Buckets**

Simple plastic buckets will suffice. The Home Depot buckets are excellent for use because they are of high quality. You will require two of them.

- **Solvents**

You can use rubbing alcohol, butane, ethanol, or even water as a solvent. It is recommended that 500 mL be used for each ounce of plant material.

- **A Breaking Stick**

Any untreated wood will suffice. As long as the branch is strong enough, you can literally find it outside your house.

This process will be aided by heavy-duty, multi-purpose rubber gloves.

- **Strainers**

You can get a coffee mesh strainer for this purpose. They are usually quite inexpensive.

- **Rice Cooker or Crock Pot**

Because this process is extremely flammable, using a stovetop is strongly discouraged and extremely dangerous. The use of a crockpot or a rice cooker will be essential for reducing the solvent.

- **Container Made of Stainless Steel**

The size of this item will be determined by the amount of oil you intend to produce. This will be used in the final dehydration step. (Recommended) A Syringe Made of Plastic

This is not required, but it will aid in the collection and storage of your RSO.

As you can see, the materials required for making RSO yourself are quite simple, and obtaining them is not only simple but also inexpensive. Once you have these items, you will be able to make as much Rick Simpson Oil as you want.

The Process

Step 1: A Simple Start

Simply place your dried cannabis plant material in the bucket. Have your solvent measured out and ready in accordance with the optimal ratio of solvent to plant material, as discussed in the supplies section. Pour the solvent slowly onto the plant matter, but not all of it — just enough to dampen it.

Step 2 Crush Time

Take your untreated wooden crushing stick and start crushing up the dampened plant material. Repeat until the plant material is finely crushed, and then add more solvent, soaking it as you crush. Continue to crush, adding more solvent as needed (the plant material should be completely soaked).

This procedure should take about 3-5 minutes. After that, pour the black oil into the other bucket. This dark oil is almost entirely THC (80+ percent)! Maintain the plant material in the bucket and add more solvent to collect the remaining (20% or so) THC in the plant. Crush for an additional 3-5 minutes.

Dump the remaining 20% of the soaked plant material into the bucket with the remaining 80% oil. Put on your heavy-duty, multi-purpose rubber gloves and throw away all plant matter. Squeeze and squish the remains as much as you can with your hands to extract as much oil as possible.

Step 3 Evaporation

You should now have a bucket full of pure THC oil with plant material floating around in it. Take out your stainless-steel container and coffee filter.

Pour the oil from the bucket through the filter and into the stainless steel container with care.

Transfer the oil from the container to your crock pot or rice cooker to begin slowly cooking off the hazardous solvents. Keep the stainless steel container handy in case you need it again.

Fill the rice cooker or crock pot halfway with oil, then turn the heat to high. Remember that the solvents are highly flammable and should not be exposed to high temperatures, so use a crockpot or rice cooker.

You will notice that the amount of liquid decreases over time as evaporation gradually removes the unwanted solvents. Continue to pour oil into the rice cooker or crock pot until all of it has been reduced. Once it has significantly reduced, add about ten drops of water to the mixture to help separate the poisonous solvents from the oils. Continue until only a small amount of solvent water remains on top of the oil.

Pick up the cooker and swirl the solvent water around and around until you can't see any more, using oven mitts to protect your hands. Turn the heat down to low right away, as the oil should never get hotter than 290 degrees Fahrenheit. Then, take out your stainless-steel container and pour the oil from the cooker into it.

Step 4: Wait, and then have fun!

Once you've gotten your oil into the stainless-steel container, you'll need to put it on a low heat to finish the evaporation process. This is where your coffee warmer or heating pad will come in handy. Leave the stainless-steel container on the warming source until all of the liquid has evaporated, leaving only pure oil. This waiting game can take 3-4 hours, but perseverance will be rewarded; you want to ensure that all solvents are long gone.

Suck up all of the oil from the container with your plastic syringe, being careful to get every drop (remember, each drop is pure THC, and thus valuable). The syringe will hold the oil, keeping it fresh and effective while also serving as an excellent applier.

All that remains is to have fun! Remember that this is a strong oil, so use caution when administering it. However, RSO is the most well-known form of cannabis extract for cancer treatment, and it is highly recommended for medical use because the oil works wonders on a variety of severe ailments. There are many people out there who merely pretend to make this stuff. So, if you want some, you should make it yourself. You can, however, do so now! Rick Simpson's legacy lives on through you.

Chapter 6

How to Make Tinctures

The Waiting Extract

Tinctures are remarkably simple to explain as well as make. Tinctures are essentially pure, liquid cannabis extracts in which alcohol is used to strip the cannabis of its THC. This potent and efficient method of medication is highly recommended for chronic pain and, as a result, medical use. The pure THC liquid is known to provide the user with the effects of cannabis within fifteen minutes of applying only a few drops under the tongue; this stuff is very potent!

By far the simplest method of extraction, as all that is required is to mix and wait. There are no safety precautions to take when making tincture, other than not using too much of the finished product. Are you ready to discover a simple cannabis extraction method? All you have to do is gather the materials and then wait for chemistry to work its magic. That's all there is to it.

Supplies Needed

Cannabis

Tinctures can be made from leaves, trimmings, or buds. The higher the quality of the plant material, as with all cannabis extracts, the better the cannabis extract. 100% Pure Grain Alcohol

Most liquor stores sell this nearly pure alcohol, known as Everclear. It is primarily used to produce various types of alcohol and should never be consumed because it contains 90 percent or more alcohol. This stuff, as you might expect, is extremely flammable!

Jar made of glass

Any glass jar will do, but it must have an airtight seal (such as Mason jars). The size of the jar will be determined by how much tincture you intend to make. Strainer and Small Funnel

These are required for transporting your tincture. A standard funnel and a coffee mesh filter will suffice. Eyedropper and Medicine Bottle

This is used for both storage and application.

In reality, making cannabis tincture requires very little effort. A bottle of Everclear costs less than ten dollars. Mason jars, small funnels, strainers, medicine jars, and eyedroppers are all readily available. The most difficult aspect of making this cannabis extract is obtaining the plant material itself.

The Process

Step 1: Make a plan.

To begin, you must determine how much tincture you intend to make. Most extracts necessitate a significant amount of cannabis plant extract, but not this one. Minimum batches can be as small as 35 ml (or 1 ounce), with a plant material ratio of 1 gram. However, the sky is the limit, and you can make as much tincture as you want using this ratio (1 gram for every 1 ounce of pure grain alcohol).

Step 2: Concoct the Concoction

This is the majority of the work. Place your cannabis plant material in a mason jar (appropriately sized for the batch, of course), and fill the jar with the specified amount of pure grain alcohol. Remember that each dose for this recipe is approximately 3-4 drops. One ounce of liquid yields approximately 24 drops, so 1 gram of plant material to 1 ounce of pure grain alcohol yields approximately six doses. Place the plant material and grain alcohol in a safe place after you've combined them. It will now be necessary to sit.

Step 3: Shake and Wait

Make sure to return to your tincture and thoroughly shake it every 5-10 days for the next 5-10 days. There is no set time limit, but this is a good starting point for first-time users. Some experienced users will soak their cannabis for weeks or even months to create a potent tincture.

Remember that the longer you soak it, the stronger it will become. Maintain vigilance and shake your tincture at least once a day.

Step 4: Keep & Enjoy

Now that it's been at least 5-10 days, your tincture is probably ready to use. However, taste it first to try and test the strength; you might want a stronger batch. If this is the case, simply replace the lid and leave the jar to sit for a while longer.

If the tincture is ready and suitable for your needs, carefully transfer the liquid medicine into a medicine bottle using your small funnel and strainer. Take your eyedropper, fill it with this potent tincture, and enjoy!

Chapter 7

How to Make Cannabutter

Cannabis to Culinary

This next cannabis product has been around for quite some time. Knowing how to make this opens up a whole new world of cannabis extracts.

Cannabutter has a nearly limitless number of applications, ranging from spreading it on toast to putting it in your coffee (perhaps unbelievably, this is very delicious). More remarkably, cannabutter is the sole foundation and key component of the wonderful world of edibles (more on that in a bit).

Cannabutter is exactly what it sounds like: cannabis combined with butter. To put it simply, the process of making it heats up the THC in the cannabis and infuses it into the butter. The heating part is especially important because simply eating cannabis raw is inefficient; the amount you would have to eat to have any noticeable effect would greatly upset your stomach and would most likely do nothing.

When cannabis is heated properly, it activates the THC through a process known as decarboxylation, which involves heating up the dormant THCA (a THC precursor) and transforming it into THC.

Cannabis smoking is essentially decarboxylation. Cannabutter is made by draining cannabinoids from plant material, activating their THC molecules, and infusing them with butter — a solvent that freezes the THC, leaving it activated within its grasp.

Safety and Such

Making this cannabis extract is very simple, and all of the materials required are typically found in your home. If not, they are common cooking utensils that can be obtained with little effort. Because this process involves heat, some precautions should be taken. They are, however, self-explanatory and mirror normal cooking precautions.

Wear long sleeves, keep a close eye on the boiling pot to avoid burning anything, keep flammable items away from the cooking surface; you know, the basics of cooking.

With just a little kitchen experience, you'll be able to make this cannabis extract. So, are you prepared? Let us begin with what you will require.

Supplies Needed

This is required for making cannabutter and requires a 1 cup butter to 12-ounce cannabis ratio.

Cannabutter is great because you can make it with your leaves, and the taste will be hidden in whatever you eat or cook with cannabutter.

Water

To the 1 cup butter to 12-ounce cannabis ratio, add 2 cups of water. For example, if you want to make cannabutter with 2 ounces of cannabis, you'll need 4 cups of butter and 8 cups of water.

Strainer made of metal

You can also use cheesecloth, but a metal strainer is more likely to be in your kitchen. This device will be used to separate cannabis from butter.

Pan of Medium Size

This is the vessel in which you will cook your cannabutter. Keep an eye on your cooking butter because burning it will ruin not only your cannabutter, but also your pan!

Bowl

A glass bowl at room temperature is recommended, but any bowl will suffice.

Isn't it strange? That is all you require. Except for the cannabis, it would not be surprising to find all of this in your own kitchen.

So, what do you think? Take those cannabis leaves you were going to throw away and head to the kitchen. Let's make some cannabis butter!

The Process

Step 1 Getting Started

First, ensure that all of your measurements are in accordance with the 2 cups of water to 1 cup of butter to 12 ounces of cannabis ratio.

Once you've gotten this all figured out, grab a medium-sized pan and add water and butter to it over medium heat. If you think you need more water to separate the butter from the pan, add more water.

Step 2: Prepare the Cannabis.

Once your butter and water are nicely simmering, add your cannabis and reduce the heat to low. Thoroughly combine. Allow the simmering pot to cook for 2-3 hours, keeping an eye on it and stirring it occasionally to prevent burning. It's a good idea to stir every 5-10 minutes.

Step 3 is to strain it.

After simmering your cannabis for 2-3 hours, making sure there is always water in the pan (if the water begins to evaporate during the previous step, make sure to add more of it accordingly), you are ready to strain it. Allow it to cool for a few minutes first. Then, while holding your bowl, carefully pour your cannabis/water/butter concoction through the metal strainer and into the bowl. You should now have a mix of water and green, oily butter.

Step 4: Place in the refrigerator, wait, and enjoy!

You're almost done. Place the bowl in the fridge and leave the cannabinoid concoction to sit overnight. A green block of butter floating on the water like moss will greet you in the morning. Remove it, dry it off, and store it in an airtight container. You can keep your cannabutter in the refrigerator for weeks before it spoils, but it will keep in the freezer for months!

Cannabutter can be spread on toast, but the flavor may be a little bitter. Dropping some in coffee, on the other hand, works really well. However, as previously stated, cannabutter's most notable feature is its role in the culinary cannabis world, also known simply as "edibles."

Bonus Tip: To make canna-oil, use the same recipe as above, but instead of butter, use vegetable oil. It is a more nutritious option. The fuller flavor of cannabutter, on the other hand, is likely to be preferred by the majority of people.

Chapter 8

How to Make Edibles, Part I: Brownies & Cookies

Now that you've got your cannabutter in the fridge, let's dive into the world of edibles. This type of cannabis extract is by far the most delicious, as the possibilities for cannabinoid-infused foods are endless. To put it simply, edibles are THC-infused foods that you can eat.

In this chapter, we'll go over the most common and beginner-friendly edibles. The basic edibles we'll look at in this chapter are ones you've probably heard of: pot brownies and weed cookies. These are the simplest edibles to prepare and are highly recommended for beginners.

Pot Brownies

Pot brownies are the most well-known of edibles, having appeared in films, television shows, and people's everyday lives. These tasty cannabis treats are ideal for occasional recreational use and provide an infusion of THC without the use of smoke.

Supplies Needed

Canna-oil/ Cannabutter

Follow the same recipe as in Chapter 7 to make canna oil, but instead of butter, use vegetable oil. For your brownies, you'll need 1 cup of cannabutter or canna oil.

A Baking Dish

This item is almost certainly already in your kitchen. A Small Stove Top Pan

You can reuse the pan from *Chapter 7:* How to Make Cannabutter.

Brownie Concoction

You can use any brownie mix you want.

A Spoon Made of Wood

This will be used to combine your brownie batter.

Eggs

You may use two eggs, but this is entirely dependent on the brownie mix you choose.

The Process

First, melt the cannabutter.

Warm your cannabutter in a small/medium stove pan until it reverts to an oil. If you overheat your cannabutter, it will burn. If you're using canna oil, you won't need to do this step because you'll already have an oil-based cannabis extract.

Once the cannabutter is melted, reduce the heat to low and turn your attention to the brownie mix.

Step 2: Prepare the Brownie Filling

Mix your brownie batter with a wooden spoon. Brownie mixes typically call for up to two eggs. Then, in the baking pan, add your cannabutter or canna oil. Once the green oil has settled on the pan's floor, pour your brownie batter directly on top of the cannabutter.

3rd Step: Bake and Enjoy

Now that you have a baking pan full of cannabutter and brownie mix, place it in a 350°F oven and set your timer for 30 minutes. Check on your brownies every ten minutes to ensure they are done.

30 minutes may not be long enough, as it has been known to take up to an hour.

When the top of the brownies becomes lightly crispy, this is a good indicator. Remove the delectable treats from the oven, allow to cool, and serve. Be cautious at first, as you should cautiously test their potency.

Weed Cookies

We'll now show you how to make another common and popular edible: the weed cookie. These, like pot brownies, are great for occasional recreational use but, like most cookies, should probably not be consumed on a regular basis. Cannabutter can be used to make any type of cookie, from sugar cookies to macadamia cookies.

Cookies are distinct in that they can be made with dried cannabis plant material rather than cannabutter or canna oil. This section will be divided into two recipes: a traditional chocolate chip cookie with dried cannabis plant material and a white chocolate chip macadamia cookie with cannabutter. Yes, they are as delectable as they sound!

The Classic Chocolate Chip Cookie with Dried Cannabis

Depending on your tolerance, you will need 14 ounces to 34 ounces of buds or trimmings.

Utensils for the Kitchen

Two medium-sized mixing bowls, a hand or electric mixer, a measuring cup, a basic measuring set, a wooden spatula or a wooden spoon, a baking sheet, and baking paper are required.

- You will need 2 cups of flour.
- Soda for Baking
- The recipe calls for 12 teaspoons.
- a pinch of salt
- You'll need 12 teaspoons of this again.
- 34 cup unsalted butter will suffice.
- One cup of brown sugar, lightly packed, is required.
- White Sugar 1/3 cup white sugar is requested.
- One tablespoon vanilla extract is required.
- Eggs You will need two eggs, one of which will be used solely for the yolk.
- Bar of Chocolate
- This must be broken up into small pieces and total 1 cup.
- A coffee grinder will suffice.

The Process

Step 1: Begin the Mix: Grease your baking pan and preheat your oven to 350 degrees. Then, using your dried cannabis and coffee bean grinder, grind your plant matter to a fine powder. Set aside the fine cannabis dust with the other dry ingredients (flour, baking soda, and salt).

Melt your unsalted butter in the microwave or on the stovetop, then combine it with white sugar and brown sugar. Mix thoroughly, then add your eggs and vanilla extract, followed by your broken-up chocolate bar.

Step 2: Drop Those Cookies: Place your cookies on a pre-greased baking sheet. This recipe will make 12-18 small cookies or 10-12 medium-sized cookies. Place your cookies in the oven for 15-20 minutes, checking them frequently to ensure they are not overdone.

Step 3: Don't Burn Your Mouth: The delectable cookies will be begging you to eat them the moment they come out of the oven. However, be patient and allow them to cool before diving in. Allow at least 5-10 minutes for them to cool before serving.

Scrumptious White Chocolate Chip Macadamia Cookie with Cannabutter

Supplies Needed

Cannabutter: You'll need 34 cups of cannabutter.

Kitchen Utensils: Two medium-sized mixing bowls, a hand or electric mixer, a measuring cup, a basic measuring set, a wooden spatula or a wooden spoon, a baking sheet, and baking paper are required.

You will need 2 1/4 cups flour.

The recipe calls for 12 teaspoons of baking soda.

a pinch of salt

12 teaspoon of this is required.

- One cup of brown sugar, lightly packed, is required.

- White Sugar 1/3 cup white sugar is requested.

- One tablespoon vanilla extract is required.

- Eggs: You will need two eggs, one full egg, and one egg just for the yolk. Chips in white chocolate

- One cup of white chocolate chips are required; however, you can add more or use less if desired.

- Macadamia Nuts: 1/2 a cup of macadamia nuts, broken into smaller pieces

The Process

This process is very similar to making cookies with dried cannabis, but don't be fooled by the similarities; there are a few minor differences to consider.

Step 1: Begin the Mix: Begin the same way you did in the previous recipe, by greasing your pan after preheating your oven to 350 degrees. Set aside your dry ingredients (flour, baking soda, and salt). Melt your cannabutter over low heat.

Once your cannabutter has melted (heat on low), combine it with the white sugar, brown sugar, and the rest of the dry ingredients.

After thoroughly mixing, add your eggs and vanilla extract.

Finally, stir in the white chocolate chips and macadamia nuts.

Step 2: Drop Those Cookies: As with the previous recipe, this one yields 12-18 small cookies or 10-12 medium-sized cookies. Place the cookies in the oven and bake for 15-20 minutes. Check them frequently and cook them for a little longer if you want crispy cookies (20-25 minutes).

Step 3: Don't Burn Your Mouth: These delectable cookies will be begging you to eat them as soon as they come out of the oven. Allow them to cool for a few minutes before diving in. Allow at least 5-10 minutes for them to cool before serving.

We learned how to make the most basic and possibly the most famous edibles in this chapter: the pot brownie and the weed cookie. However, the culinary options for cannabutter vary greatly, and we will continue to explore the "cannabinoid meets culinary arts" story in the next chapter as we move into more complicated dishes. We'll show you how to use edibles to make breakfast, lunch, dinner, and dessert in the following chapter!

Chapter 9

How to make Edibles,

Part II:

Further Exploration

We only scratched the surface of the wondrous world of edibles in the previous chapter; brownies and cookies are just the beginning! In this chapter, we will delve deeper into the cannabis culinary world by providing a full day's worth of meals: breakfast, lunch, dinner, and dessert.

Using cannabutter and canna-oils opens up a world of culinary possibilities, so covering all edibles would be like entering a never-ending book. We won't be able to cover every recipe, but our goal is to get you acquainted with cooking with cannabutter or canna oil. Once you've mastered that, the possibilities for edibles are virtually limitless.

A hearty breakfast is essential for a good start to any day, and we're going to show you how to make a delicious breakfast dish: the Belgian Waffle.

"Good Morning!"-The Cannabis Belgian Waffle

Supplies Needed

Waffle Maker

This kitchen tool is required for making waffles easily and correctly.

- Cannabutter (approximately 1/2 cups)
- a pair of bowls
- One small and one medium bowl are required.
- Traditional Egg Beater

You can do this by hand, but having a machine makes things even easier.

WOODEN SPOONS

- A small stovetop pan for mixing
- This will make things easier for you.
- Two eggs will suffice, and the yolks will be separated from the whites.
- Two cups milk, make sure it's warmed before using.
- Five tablespoons white sugar

- 1 1/2 teaspoon vanilla extract; 2 3/4 cup flour
- a pinch of salt
- A teaspoon or a generous pinch will suffice. (Optional) Syrup from maple trees

To make this an even more enjoyable experience, have pure maple syrup on hand to add as desired. It is not, however, required.

The Process

To begin, take a small pan, turn your stove top burner to low heat, and place cannabutter inside the pan. You should have melted cannabutter in about ten minutes. When you're mixing, this will make your life easier. Next, separate the yolks from the whites of your eggs; both parts will be used in this recipe.

In a medium-sized mixing bowl, thoroughly combine the warm milk, flour, sugar, cannabutter, egg yolks, vanilla extract, and salt with a wooden spoon. Make sure your batter is consistent.

Now, in the smaller bowl, beat your egg whites with your egg beater. Allow this to sit for at least 3-5 minutes before adding it to your ingredients in the medium bowl. Allow for a 40-minute resting period.

Step 2: Cook and eat!

Prepare your waffle iron with oil and sufficient heat. Pour your batter into the waffle iron and cook until golden brown. Allow your waffles to cool before serving, and you're done! Relax now and, if desired, drizzle some pure maple syrup on your cannabis-infused Belgian waffles to start your day on a high note!

"Good Afternoon!"

Homemade Cannabis

Macaroni and Cheese

Supplies Needed

- Cannabutter Use 1/2 cup of your favorite cannabutter.
- 1/2 cup shredded cheddar cheese and 1/2 cup shredded mozzarella cheese are required.
- a medium-sized frying pan
- This is essential.
- Six cups of water will suffice.
- Pasta

Use small pasta shells for this recipe. One standard-sized box will suffice.

- One tablespoon black pepper

- Strainer for Pasta

For this dish, a medium or large pasta strainer will suffice.

- 12 cup heavy whipping cream

This dish is ideal for a filling lunch and can be served as a small side dish or as the main course due to its cheesy deliciousness. You can also add bacon if you want; cook two pieces of bacon, mince them, and add them to the final dish.

The Process

Getting Started is the first step.

Bring water to a boil in a medium-sized saucepan. Turn the heat down to 34 degrees Fahrenheit and add your pasta. 8-10 minutes in a preheated oven. After that, strain your pasta through a strainer and rinse with hot water from your sink. Allow no more than 2 minutes for the pasta to drain.

Step 2: Put Everything Together.

Now, take your cannabutter and place it in the empty pan. To properly melt the cannabutter, reduce the heat to low. When it has melted, add your pasta and thoroughly mix it in. Combine the cheese, cream, and black pepper in a mixing bowl. Stir vigorously for 3-5 minutes.

Step 3: Allow to cool before serving.

Allow your mac and cheese to cool for 5 minutes before serving. This is a delicious side dish for any lunch. To make your mac and cheese a main course, add bacon: two cooked pieces of cooked bacon, minced, and added to the final stirring process.

"Good Evening!"

Red Mashed Potatoes with Cannabis

Supplies Needed

- 1/2 cup to 3/4 cup cannabutter, depending on preference
- Garlic is a herb: you'll need about 2-3 cloves.
- Salt one tbsp, Pepper one tbsp, Red Potatoes because these are usually quite small, a size of 10-12 is recommended.
- Large frying pan: this is going to be your primary tool.
- Wooden Spoon: for the purpose of stirring.
- 1/2 cup heavy whipping cream Strainer A traditional pasta strainer will suffice.

The Process

Step 1: Bring the Taters to a boil.

Bring water to a boil in a large pan. Rinse and cut your red potatoes into fourths (without peeling), then carefully place them in a pot of boiling water. Reduce the heat to 34 degrees Celsius, which is halfway between medium and high.

Cook potatoes for 10-15 minutes, stirring occasionally, or until a fork easily pierces them. While you're waiting, finely chop your garlic. Place the potatoes in a strainer and return the large pan to the stovetop, reducing the heat to 1/4, between low and medium.

Step 2: Blend It Up

To begin, melt the majority of your cannabutter. Then, add the minced garlic and stir it into the cannabutter for about 3 minutes. Take your steaming red potatoes and add them to the pot.

Begin mashing with the wooden spoon, stirring as you go.

Continue to stir in the heavy whipping cream, gradually adding salt and pepper. Continue to stir until the potatoes are clearly mashed and have a gentle fluffiness to them.

Step 3: Let it cool and enjoy it.

Allow your cannabis-infused mashed potatoes to cool for 5-8 minutes to allow the remaining flavors to blend into the flavor.

Serve as a side dish for any appropriate dinner!

"Goodnight!"

Cannabis Toffee Crumble for Ice Cream Dessert

Supplies Needed

- Cannabutter
- For this recipe, use a quarter cup.
- Thermometer Made of Candy
- You can purchase one of these at Walmart or on Amazon. They are inexpensive, costing between $10 and $15.
- Salt
- It's only a pinch.
- One cup granulated sugar
- One teaspoon vanilla extract. One teaspoon chocolate chips
- Prepare 1 cup of these ahead of time.
- 12 cup chopped walnuts
- Medium Saucepot

- This is going to be your primary tool.
- Pan for Baking
- A cookie sheet will suffice.
- Wooden Spoons
- For agitation.
- Only two tablespoons of ice water are required.

The Process

The first step is to make the candy.

First, grease and set aside a cookie sheet. Next, take a medium saucepan and heat it over medium heat on the stove.

Combine the sugar, cannabutter, and one tablespoon of ice water, reserving the remaining tablespoon for later.

Cook for 12-15 minutes on medium, keeping a close eye on it and frequently stirring the liquid candy with a wooden spoon. Your candy is ready when the candy thermometer reads 300 degrees.

Step 2: Dump, Crack and Have Fun.

Place the scalding candy mix on a greased cookie sheet.

When you have all of your candy on the cookie sheet, you will notice that it is quickly solidifying. When it has hardened, sprinkle it with the remaining tablespoon of ice water, spreading it around the surface of the hard candy.

This will cause the toffee to crack. Finish the day off right by carefully sprinkling some vanilla bean ice cream with the warm cannabis toffee.

Snacking on butters and sugars can be unhealthy in the long run, so these methods are better suited for occasional recreational use. However, if your health permits, they are great, tasty alternatives for cannabis medicating.

What did we learn from the above-mentioned fundamentals? We discovered that cooking with cannabutter is largely similar to cooking with regular butter. Find some more recipes that call for butter or oil; these are usually ideal for making cannabis edibles.

Chapter 10

How to Make Hash

History of Hashish

Hashish has a long history, making it one of the oldest cannabis extracts on the market. Hashish dates back to around 900 A.D. in Arabia, but some legends claim that it has been around for thousands of years longer. A story about assassins using this early cannabis extract made its way to Europe around 1200 AD, and soon after, early scientists began investigating its medicinal properties.

Pharmaceutical companies began to control the market at the end of the nineteenth century. Cannabis was considered an outlaw at the time.

Now, in the twenty-first century, cannabis has regained the recognition that it had lost so long ago, and its presence in the medical world is regaining strength. Even for recreational purposes, it has become one of the most popular ways to unwind. Hash is one of the simplest extracts to make, and there are literally hundreds of different approaches to collecting the "golden dust."

The methods for obtaining hash have changed over time, but the hash itself has not. Hash is THC extracted from the plant by stripping the trichomes, or little white hairs, of their THC crystals, resulting in a pure and effective way to medicate, or simply a great way to kick back and relax. In this chapter, we will go over some of the most fundamental methods for creating hashes, as they are the simplest and fastest. Are you prepared to carry this ancient cannabis tradition forward?

Harvest Hash

This method, also known as "Finger Hash," is about as simple as it gets when it comes to hashing. However, there is a catch to this extract method, as it is heavily dependent on harvest. When harvesting a plant, the trimming process occurs immediately after the plant is pulled or after it has completely dried.

The goal is to clean up the buds, removing any leafy vegetation from the valuable buds. While going through this laborious process, you will notice an immediate reward: golden-brown gunk will begin to accumulate on your clippers and fingers.

Using a paper clip, remove the sticky substance from the clipper blades and roll the stickiness off your fingers. This will start to form into a small ball. What do you think? You have just made hash! You can smoke this pure hash over a nice bowl of green flowers for fun or vaporize it for a great medical alternative. As long as you find a good harvest, this hashish almost produces itself.

Blend up some Hash

All you'll need for this method is dried cannabis, a blender, two glass jars, a silkscreen, and a coffee mesh strainer. Also, have some ice cubes on hand. There is no danger involved, so no special precautions are required. Another quick and easy way to make hashish is to blend some hash. This is how it's done!

The Process

Step 1: Mix it all together.

Add the dried plant material and ice cubes to your blender (the more material, the more hash, so there is no set amount). Add water (enough to soak the plant material) and blend until smooth. Blend for another 1 minute or so to break down the fiber.

Step 2: Strain and Set It.

Pour the vibrant green liquid through the silkscreen and into one of the glass jars now that you have a cannabis smoothie. Allow your green liquid to settle for 20-30 minutes.

Step 3: Finally, relax and enjoy.

You should now see the hash settling at the bottom of the jar. Remove about two-thirds of the surfacing water before adding more. This will help to clear up your hash. Remove the majority of the water from the settled hash by dumping it out, then strain the remainder through the coffee mesh filter and into your other jar. You now have some tasty hashish!

The Classic Screen Hash

This is most likely the most popular method. All you need are some cannabis flowers or trimmings, a small mesh screen, a credit card, and a large mirror (this will be used to catch the trichomes). There are no safety precautions to take when doing this. This method does not produce as much hash as the others, but it is the least expensive and most convenient.

The Process

Getting Started is the first step.

Place your small mesh screen over the glass mirror. Then, add your marijuana to the screen.

Step 2: Slide Your Card & Have Fun!

Slide your credit card back and forth across the screen, essentially pushing the flowers, or trimmings, around. As you proceed gently with this action, the THC from the trichomes will begin to scrape off. Your glass will be completely covered in the hash in no time.

However, those flowers or trimmings will still contain a significant amount of THC, so don't throw them away. These are ideal for making cannabutter, as discussed in previous chapters.

In this chapter, we only touched on a few of the most popular hashing methods. Nonetheless, there are numerous other, more advanced hashing methods and forms. In the following chapter, we'll look at one of the most popular of these: bubble hash.

Chapter 11

How to Make Bubble Hash

Bubble Hash gets its name from the "bubble bag" in which it is made.

Bubble hash, like regular hash, is a pure form of the cannabinoids extracted from the trichomes. The method itself gives bubble hash a distinct appearance, and when you smoke it, it is known to bubble — another quality that contributes to its name. While regular hash is typically a golden brown color, bubble hash can be pitch black, luscious green, soft yellow, or the traditional golden brown. Bubble hash also comes in various textures, depending on the cannabis strain.

Bubble hash can be enjoyed in a variety of ways, including in a water pipe or by adding it to joints.

It can be used recreationally or medicinally, depending on your medical condition. Some medical conditions permit the use of vapours, but it is usually safe to say that avoiding smoke when pre-existing health conditions exist is prudent.

Bubble Hash is one of the most natural methods of producing hash because the solvent is simply ice water. Aside from the specialized bubble bag kit, everything else you'll need to make this cannabis extract is readily available in most kitchens. This cannabis extract method is also extremely safe, requiring no special precautions.

So, are you up for some bubble hash? Let's start with the materials.

Supplies Needed

Cannabis flowers or trimmings will suffice, but trimmings are preferred because this method turns trash into gold. Your cannabis product must be frozen. You'll need four small, traditional sandwich bags full of frozen cannabis — or about four ounces — for this recipe.

Kit for Making Bubble Bags

The most basic kit consists of five bags: a main, working bag, and four-micron bags ranging in size from 23 microns to larger.

Each bag will produce a unique type of bubble hash.

Blender

If you want to mix by hand, you can use a wooden spoon or a traditional egg beater. A mixing drill used in construction when mixing mortar and cement is one of the best mixers for this recipe, but it is not widely available. This is the best tool to use if you have one of these. However, make certain that it is completely clean!

Buckets

It's just two 5 gallon buckets. The sturdy orange buckets from Home Depot are ideal for making bubble hash.

Spoons

A regular tablespoon will suffice.

Water and ice

Two small bags of ice will suffice, and make sure the water is cold and, preferably, filtered.

This method of producing hash takes some time, but the rewards are plentiful and well worth the effort.

The Process

A solid foundation is essential for any project. Make sure you have plenty of ice and water on hand. Have your two buckets ready as well. Add about three healthy scoops of ice to one bucket. Insert your main "working" bubble bag into this bucket, followed by more ice and your frozen, dried cannabis plant material. Add more ice and water until all of the plant material is submerged and soaked.

Step 2: Combine and mash the ingredients.

You will now have one bucket with your main bag, which will be filled with cannabis, water, and ice. The other bucket should be empty (we'll use it shortly). Take your mixer (egg beater, wooden spoon, or mixing drill) and thoroughly mix plant material in ice water for 10-15 minutes. Allow it to settle for 10-20 minutes after vigorous mixing and smashing.

Step 3: Prepare Your Bags.

You should now have a bucket of ice water and cannabis. It is now time to prepare your second bucket. Make your four bubble bags.

The smallest micron bag should be placed in the bucket first, followed by the next size up inside that, then the next inside that, and so on.

Your second bucket will contain four bags.

Step 4: Empty the main bag.

Your first main bag is ready to be retrieved. Pull the main bag up through the murky water, slowly and softly shaking the bag. Make certain that all of the water has been strained through the main bag. The plant material stripped of its cannabinoids should be left inside the main bag, and the five-gallon bucket should be full of murky-looking water. Pour this water into the second bucket, along with your four-micron bags.

Step 5: Hash Layers

Take your first bag and shake it slowly to separate it from the others.

When you remove the first bag, you should notice that some hash has accumulated at the bottom of the filter. Collect this gold with your spoon, making sure to place this creamy substance on a safe surface. Repeat the process with the next bag, and then the next, and then the next.

At the bottom of each bag, there should be more bubbly goodness. Remove the hash with each yield and set it aside. After you've removed all of your bags, the water solvent should be depleted of all cannabinoids, and you should have four different piles of creamy bubble hash on the surface. Your task has been completed.

Step 6: Allow to dry and then enjoy.

After allowing your hash to dry for about 15-20 hours, you will notice that the once creamy substance has transformed into a more traditional looking hash.

Depending on the strain you used to make your bubble hash, each pile will be different. These little piles, on the other hand, are ready for consumption. Keep each little pile separate and apply to any joint or vaporizer, depending on how you intend to use your bubble hash. Now sit back, relax, and watch your hash bubble.

It is finally time to relax after all of your hard work.

Chapter 12

How to Make Kief

The oldest form of Hash

Kief is the first type of hash, and this cannabis extract is known as "dry hash." Hash is typically clumpy, almost brown and sugar-like, or oil, whereas kief is a pure green powder — a collection of cannabinoids in their most basic form. In other words, kief is hash in its most basic form.

Kief, like most cannabis products, can be used either medically or recreationally. In comparison to smoking, vaporizing this extract proves to be a great medical alternative. There are two ways to obtain kief, one of which is so simple that we call it the "kill-two birds with one stone technique." However, before we get into making kief, the real magic of kief is the various ways it can be smoked, so we will first look at some of these traditional methods.

Using Kief

Sprinkling the green dust into a joint or onto a pipe load is a popular way to use kief. Some people prefer to smoke it pure with a screen through a water pipe to open up the flavors. Kief can also be vaporized by adding it to a vaporizer or pouring it into an e-cig liquid cartridge.

Another way to use kief is to press it into hash. Simply grab some parchment paper and a hair straightener to get started. Fill a piece of parchment paper with kief, fold it, and press it with a hair straightener (on medium heat) for 5 seconds to make a hash. This method of generating hash is far from as efficient as the methods discussed earlier in this book. It is, however, one of the simplest ways to use kief.

Kief has also made its way into the culinary world, where it is a key ingredient in cannabutter formulas and can be added to dry edible recipes to boost potency or replace large amounts of unrefined plant material.

Now that you've got some great ideas, let's look at two ways to make this ancient cannabis extract. One is simple, and the kief will accumulate as you roll cannabis joints over time. The other requires more cannabis as well as more effort. It does, however, produce mountains of kief. We'll start with the first method called the "kill-two-birds-with-one-stone technique" or the grinder method.

Killing Two Birds With One Stone Technique

A.K.A The Grinder Method

Every time you roll a joint or break up cannabis flowers with your fingers, you've come into contact with kief — that crystal-like, green powder on your fingertips. However, collecting kief from your fingers while rolling a joint would be ineffective. Fortunately for us, a tool makes rolling joints easier and collects kief for later use — hence the technique's name. All you'll need is some cannabis and a kief grinder with three chambers.

Use your three-chamber kief grinder every time you break up cannabis to roll a joint or for any other reason. Insert your unbroken cannabis flowers into the top chamber. Put the lid on and start grinding.

Then, unscrew your grinder to reveal the second chamber.

This is where you'll keep your chopped-up cannabis for rolling joints, water pipe hits, or whatever else you want to do with the cannabis.

This is where the kief comes in. There is another chamber, the third and lowest one, and when you unscrew it, you will notice a steady buildup of kief inside. A consistent smoker can accumulate up to a half gram of kief in a week — all by smoking cannabis!

Dry Kief

This method is a little more involved, but it yields a kief that is better suited for culinary applications. You can use this kief in soups or even ice cream. In fact, you can use this dry iced kief in any dish. Let's gather some supplies before we begin.

Supplies Needed

- Cannabis

You'll need between one ounce and 1 1/2 ounces of dried cannabis plant material.

Baking Sheet; a standard baking sheet will suffice.

Cookie Sheet Paper is another name for parchment paper.

- Ice Cubes

A small bowl of dried ice (about 12 ounces).

- Bag of Bubbles

A gallon bubble bag with a 120-micron mesh screen will suffice.

- A dish that can withstand heat

A ramekin from custards or other baked goods will suffice.

- A scraper; It is sufficient to use a credit card.

Now that we have everything we need, let's get started on our dry iced kief!

The Process

Step 1: Crush the cannabis.

It is recommended that you do this by hand because you will save a lot of kief this way. Break up all of your marijuana and place it in your bubble bag.

Step 2: Sift and ice it.

Hold your bubble bag full of cannabis above the parchment paper on the inside of your baking sheet. Fill the bubble bag halfway with dry ice and gently shake to sift the kief onto the baking sheet and parchment paper.

Step 3: Gather It and Bake It.

You'll notice a lot of kief on your parchment paper now. Gather all of your kief with your scraper and place it in your ramekin.

Preheat the oven to 250°F and bake the kief for no more than 20 minutes. Remove your kief with care and add it to any dish of your choice!

Following our exploration of some methods for obtaining the most ancient cannabis extract available, kief, we would like to conclude this chapter with what the future holds. As we enter the twenty-first century, new discoveries and breakthroughs have entered the world of cannabis, the most recent of which is known as rosin, the cannabis innovation that gave rise to the dab culture.

Chapter 13

How to Make Rosin & "Do a Dab"

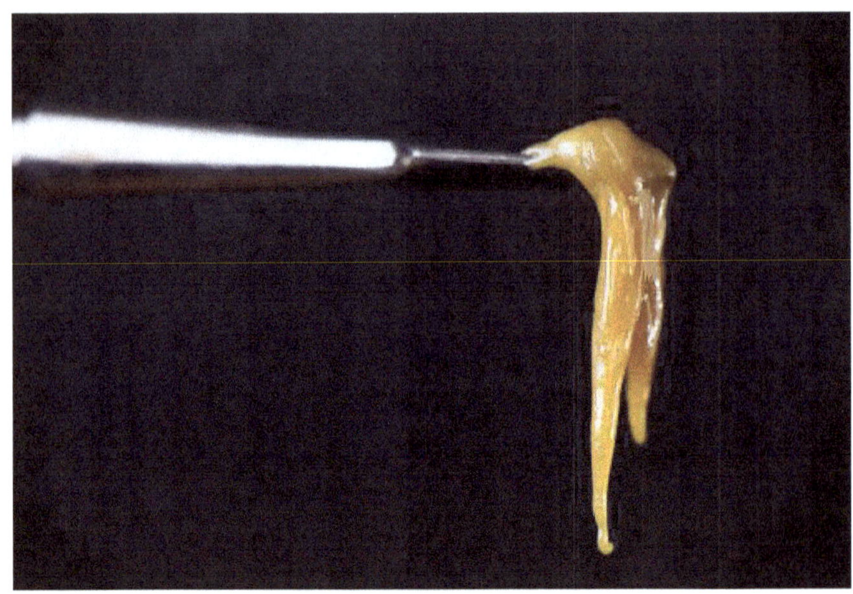

The Superhero Hashish

Although dabs have grown in popularity in recent years, the potent cannabis extract known as rosin has been on the menu since the 1960s. However, today's dab, or more specifically, rosin, is far more potent than any previous version of this derivative. Modern cannabis extracting technology and instruments have resulted in the development of non-solvent cannabinoid oils, giving rise to this superhero hash: rosin.

The cannabis extract, which can contain up to 90 percent

THC, has a superhero-like backstory, as it was the result of ten years of research in a laboratory somewhere in British Columbia, Canada.

Long before Americans, Canadian scientists had their sights set on the enchantment that accompanies cannabis.

Now that the cannabis craze has spread to the United States, more pure and clean forms of cannabinoids are in demand.

Rosin, also known as the dab, first made its way into the United States in 2010. Upon its arrival, it quickly established its fame via a laboratory in North America, claiming a popularity currently unrivaled by any other extract.

This high-powered, solvent-free hash oil, like all cannabis products, can be used for recreational or medical purposes; however, if smoking is harmful to your health, this one is recommended primarily for recreational use. The potency of the pure cannabis oil extract far outperforms any formal BHO or Bubble Hash you've ever tried.

With that said, it is strongly advised that only senior smokers use rosin, and one should exercise extreme caution when dabbing. If you do not pay attention to the strength and power of rosin, you may find yourself in trouble.

A too-potent dab or rosin dose will have you on the ground — literally!

Safety and Such

Although this superhero hash oil was created in a lab, there is a method we will look at that makes producing rosin easier than you might think. Before you start, make sure you're in a place where there's no carpet or flammable materials (like a garage).

To protect your fingers from hot oil, put on rubber gloves. This method of extract is entirely solvent-free, making it simple to prepare.

However, making a large amount of this oil necessitates a large amount of cannabis, and rosin is always made with the flower. After you've learned what comes next, you'll be ready to take a dab, but first, let's make some rosin.

Supplies Needed

Straightening Iron, that's correct. This is what we will be using to make our dabs. Parchment paper, also known as cookie sheets, is a nonstick baking paper and Cannabis.

Any dab should, as previously stated, be made with the flower itself.

Despite having such a complicated history in the laboratory, it is interesting to note how simple it is to make this cannabis extract oil at home!

The Process

Wrap your cannabis flower in parchment paper and heat your hair straightener to medium.

Step 2 is to press it.

Clamp the hair straightener tightly around the flower, which is encased by the parchment paper. Repeat 2-3 times for a total of 5 seconds.

A golden oil will begin to gather around the edges of the parchment paper.

Step 3: Relax and enjoy!

When you unfold the parchment paper, you'll see a smashed cannabis flower with yellow-golden oil surrounding it.

Remove the smashed bud once it has cooled and enjoy your fresh rosin oil!

Rosin, like traditional hashish, can be added to a bowl of green or vaporized; the latter is preferred when using for medicinal purposes. This new-age extract has also developed its own application method: the dab.

Now that you've made your delectable rosin, we'll show you how to properly "take a dab," as this is the most authentic and exciting way to begin your rosin journey.

Dabbing

Again, we'll emphasize the potency of a dab, as even a dab the size of a sweat bead can be highly effective — just be careful not to overdo it! You will only need a few items to enjoy a ride on "dab mountain truly."

Supplies Needed

An Oil Rig Made of Glass

This specialized piece of glassware, also known as a Dab Rig, is available at any head shop, dispensary, or online. It is essentially a water pipe, but instead of a glass bowl, it has a joint attachment into which you insert a glass nail — which you heat very hot and apply your dab to. When Dabbing, another glass attachment known as the dome is wrapped around the nail. A massive Butane Torch

This must be large enough to accommodate the size of the "nail" on your glass oil rig. Dabber

This is the tool you'll use to dab your dab, or rosin, onto the glass nail. They are available in glass or metal, with metal being preferred by cannabis enthusiasts. They resemble small metal pens but lack the actual pen.

You could apply your dab with a paper clip, but this is not recommended.

The two specialized items in the preceding list, the Glass Oil Rig and the Dabber, are usually purchased together when you buy a Dab Rig Set.

Aside from these three tools, you'll need your preferred Rosin oil concentrate. OK! Let's "Dabb" it!

The Process

The First Step: Getting Started

Fill your glass oil rig with water and insert the glass nail into the rig's attachment, known as the joint.

Heat your nail with your torch until it turns orange, making sure to keep the torch flame away from you and your glass rig.

Now, wrap your dome attachment piece around the nail.

Allow the nail to cool for 10-30 seconds to avoid completely burning the oil and to achieve a full flavor. However, if you wait too long, your nail will not burn the oil. When you get a brand new dab Rig Set, this step will take a few tries to figure out.

2nd Step: Separate

Using your dabber, separate a small bead of rosin oil. Snag the oil by the edge so the dab will easily fall off your dabber.

Step 3: Have fun!

Suck air slowly through your water pipe while placing the rosin on the hot nail. This will instantly vaporize, and you will have a mouthful of delicious cannabinoid smoke in no time.

Remove your dome piece as soon as possible so that it does not become stuck to your rig. Now, relax and enjoy the ride!

This new method of consumption has taken the cannabis world by storm.

With the discovery of rosin and the advent of the dab, cannabis users all over the world have discovered a new way to use small amounts of cannabis material to feel their wonders powerfully.

With the nineteenth century, the early popularity of hashish faded, and it appeared that the age of cannabis extracts had come to an end.

These two innovations, on the other hand, have resurrected it and paved the way for science and cannabis to combine thoroughly.

It's exciting to see where the future is going with the introduction of rosin and methods like dabbing. It's exciting to think that we're only at the start of the cannabis extract renaissance.

Chapter 14

Looking Forward to the Future

Cannabis extracts have progressed significantly. As we have seen in this book, they date back to ancient times and once took center stage in the medical field in certain cultures. With the arrival of the twentieth century came the colossal pharmaceutical drug companies, which entirely outlawed the healing cannabis plant.

Cannabis is slowly but steadily being reintroduced into the medical field and society as a whole. The once-despised drug is now recognized for what it has always been: a healing plant.

With its recent legalization in a number of states, research into this medical marvel has finally been able to flourish, resulting in many wonderful innovations such as cannabis extracts for us to enjoy.

In this book, we took you on a journey through the cannabis extract kitchen, where we discovered wonders ranging from ancient extracts like Kief and Hash to more modern extracts like Bubble Hash and Rosin. We smoked BHO, ate a four-course meal of Cannabutter and Edibles, and relaxed with some potent Tinctures. Finally, we wanted to educate and teach you how to make cannabis extracts. But why is that?

As science strolls through the cannabis garden at its leisure, ground-breaking discoveries and stories woven from miracles have emerged. Nature carries perfection somewhere in her bosom; all we have to do is seek it sincerely and without judgment. That is why we have given you this book.

Cannabis appears to hold the key to various ailments, both mental and physical, and having the ability to create this medicine is something we believe everyone should have. Cannabis has only recently begun to share her story as minds begin to blossom.

www.ingramcontent.com/pod-product-compliance
Lightning Source LLC
LaVergne TN
LVHW020608200726
843509LV00001B/24